HOW IT'S MADE
MATZAH

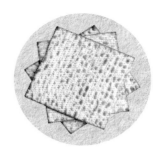

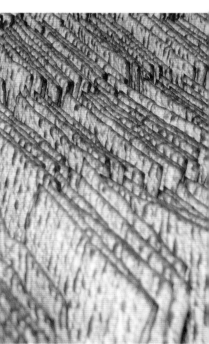

by Allison Ofanansky • Photographs by Eliyahu Alpern

Springfield, NJ • Jerusalem

We would like to thank the many people who shared their time and knowledge with us:

Gita and Rony Bar-El and The Way Inn Hotel, Tzfat Israel for hosting the seder shown on pages 4–5, http://www.thewayinn.co.il
Ronen and the Or Haganuz matzah bakery, Or Haganuz Israel shown on pages 8–14, http://www.orhaganuzwinery.com
The Rabbinic Community Association of Israel which sponsored the women's matzah making event shown on pages 15 & 16, http://www.commrabbis.com
Roy Wolf, Matzot Aviv, Bnei Brak, Israel of the matzah factory shown on pages 18–21, www.matzotaviv.com
Poster of matzah machine on page 18 from American Heritage Haggadah, courtesy of Gefen Publishing House
Canaan Gallery, Tzfat Israel for the handwoven matzah cover page 22, https://www.canaan-gallery.com
Batya Erdstein, Israel who made the seder plates on pages 3, 24 & 26, www.israelceramics.com
The publisher wishes to credit the following sources of additional photographs and illustrations:
Aluma Mishulami for the photos of Batya Erdstein
Andy Collins for the photo of the chickens on page 25, www.extremekayaker.com
Passover carpet by Moshe Castel on page 4
From the Venice Haggadah, published by Israel ben Daniel Ha-Zifroni in 1609 on page 29
Sheva Chaya Servetter, Sheva Chaya Gallery, Tzfat, Israel, http://www.shevachaya.com who made and photographed the glass cups on page 31.
Shutterstock: back cover: wheat grain: Ines Behrens-Kunkel, front cover, 14: matzos with silver bowl: Natushm, 1 matzah: Arkady Mazor, 3 matzah: Natushm,
6 matzah and plate: Tomertu, 7 wheat: Denis Vrublevski, hands: Sethislav, flour: M. Unal Ozmen, mixing bowl: Endeavor, measuring cup: Danny Smythe,
14 matzos with silver bowl: Natushm, 25 horseradish bowl: Tim UR, wine: Gresei, wheat: Inacio Pires, 27 crayons: Bogdan Ionescu,
30 apples, walnuts: Maks Narodenko, dried fruit: Olga Popova, 31 grapes: Valentyn Volkov, 32 maze: jelisua88, matzah: Julia Khelmer.

Apples & Honey Press
An imprint of Behrman House and Gefen Publishing House
Behrman House, 11 Edison Place, Springfield, New Jersey 07081
Gefen Publishing House Ltd, 6 Hatzvi Street, Jerusalem 94386, Israel
www.applesandhoneypress.com

Text copyright © 2017 by Allison Ofanansky
Photographs copyright © 2017 by Eliyahu Alpern, except as otherwise noted
ISBN 978-1-68115-524-1

Library of Congress Cataloging-in-Publication Data

Names: Ofanansky, Allison, author. | Alpern, Eliyahu, photographer.
Title: How it's made matzah / by Allison Ofanansky ; photographs by
   Eliyahu Alpern.
Description: Springfield, New Jersey : Apples & Honey Press , [2016] |
   Grades 4–6.
Identifiers: LCCN 2016001380 | ISBN 9781681155241
Subjects: LCSH: Matzos—Juvenile literature. | Passover cooking—Juvenile
   literature.
Classification: LCC TX739.2.P37 O33 2016 | DDC 641.5676437—dc23
LC record available at https://lccn.loc.gov/2016001380

Design by Elynn Cohen • Edited by Amanda Cohen
Printed in the United States of America • 9 8 7 6 5 4 3 2 1

Every year

on the first night of Passover, Jewish families and friends gather together for the seder meal.

The seder plate and a stack of matzah sit in the center of the table. For the whole week of Passover we will eat matzah. Did you ever wonder HOW matzah is made?

Growing the wheat

Mixing the dough

Eating the matzah together

Rolling out the dough

Baking the matzah

Let's find out . . .

3

But first . . . what is Passover?

Passover, Pesach פֶּסַח in Hebrew, is a holiday celebrated in the spring. It commemorates Moses leading the Israelites out of slavery, from Egypt to the Promised Land.

Passover is a celebration of our freedom.

Nissan

Passover begins on the 15th day of the Hebrew month of Nissan. In Israel the holiday lasts 7 days; outside Israel an 8th day is often celebrated.

15	16	17	18	19	20	21	22

What does "freedom" mean to YOU?

Matzah is made from just two ingredients: flour and water. Most matzah is made from wheat flour but it can also be made from rye, barley, spelt or oat flour.

Matzah must be made in **18** minutes or less

Matzah—the ultimate fast food

Why do we eat matzah on Passover? To help us remember when the Israelites left Egypt. They had to leave so quickly, they didn't have time to let their bread rise. Matzah looks like a kind of flat cracker. It is unleavened.

What does "unleavened" mean?

Unleavened dough does not rise. To be kosher for Passover, matzah must be made very quickly—in less than 18 minutes—to ensure it doesn't have time to rise even a tiny bit.

"The whole process of making matzah—from the time the grain is harvested until the matzah comes out of the oven—must be carefully watched, to make sure it never starts to rise."

–Roy Wolf, *matzah maker*

Grain

Cooled water

Kosher-for-
Passover flour

What do we need to make matzah?

Mixing bowl or
mixing machine

Rolling pin

VERY hot oven

Hole-making tool

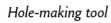

Handmade Matzah

Some matzah is made by hand in a special bakery.

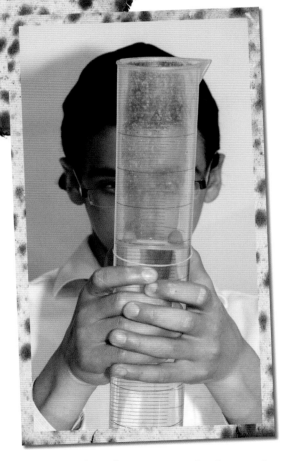

A matzah maker measures the flour and cool spring water and mixes them together.

Once the water touches the flour, the countdown begins!

Every few minutes someone announces how much time has passed so as not to go over the 18-minute time limit. The workers sing to remind themselves of the mitzvah of making matzah for Passover.

They knead the dough quickly by hand and using a steel bar.

Take a closer look

לשם מצות מצווה

Sign in matzah workshop:
L'shem matzot mitzvah
*For the sake of the
commandment of matzah*

They cut the dough into small pieces and then roll each piece into a thin circle.

Take a closer look

Checking that matzah dough is the right consistency

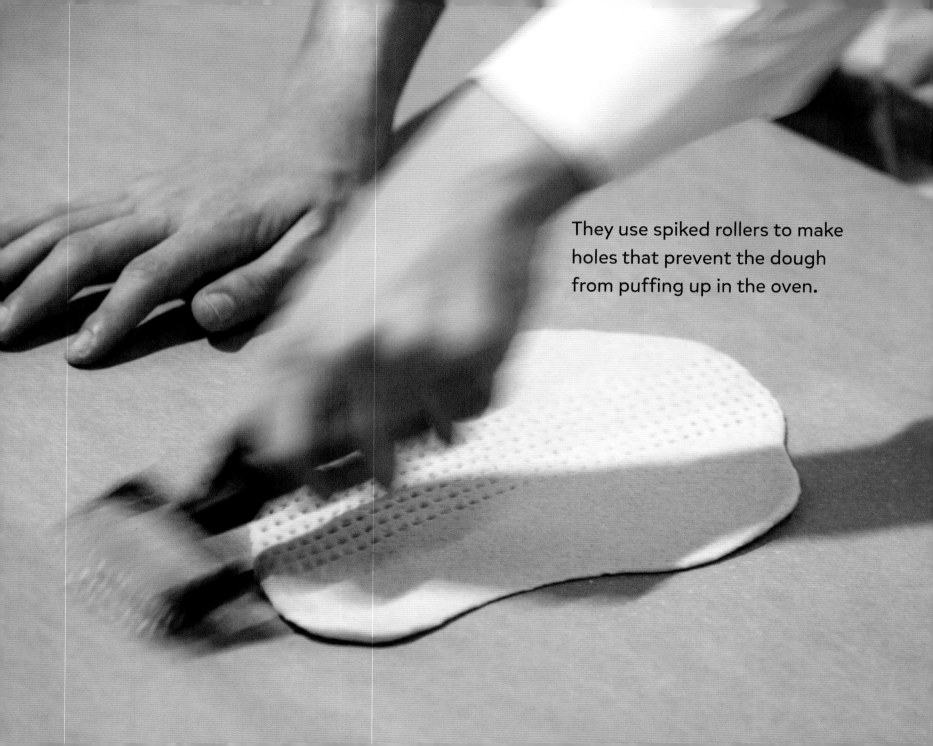

They use spiked rollers to make holes that prevent the dough from puffing up in the oven.

The team works together to get the
matzah done on time.

Using long poles, the matzah makers put the unbaked dough into a very hot oven.

Within a few minutes they take it out and set it on a rack to cool.

After each batch, matzah makers clean the entire work area and all the tools so no bits of dough are left. Any dough left past the 18-minute time limit must be thrown away.

Now the matzah is finished!

"Making matzah teaches us to work together. It is not possible to make matzah alone."

—Ronen, matzah maker

Take a closer look

Freshly baked matzah

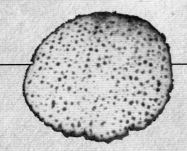

Make your own matzah!

1. Preheat the oven to 450°F.

2. Pour 3 cups of flour into a bowl.

3. Add 1 cup of cool water.

4. Start watching the clock! You only have 18 minutes from start to finish.

5. Quickly mix and knead the flour and water into a smooth ball of dough. This should take 3–5 minutes.

What matzah-making job would **YOU** most like to do?

"I put happy thoughts into the dough, so the matzah will taste good!"

–Rivka Mor Yosef,
(participant in community matzah making)

6. Roll the dough out thinly.
7. Poke holes all over with a fork.
8. Put the matzah on a baking tray and bake for 2–3 minutes.
9. You can also bake matzah on a domed pan over a hot fire.
10. Enjoy!

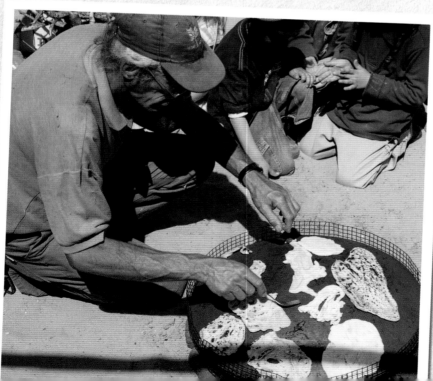

"Every job is equally important in making the matzah kosher for Passover."
—Zev Padway,
community matzah baker

17

Factory Made Matzah

About 150 years ago, matzah bakers started using machines. At first, some rabbis said only hand-made matzah was kosher for Passover. Eventually most accepted machine-made matzah.

This poster from 1855 shows an early machine used to roll out matzah.

Computerized matzah factory

Today there are modern factories where machines do almost every stage of the matzah making. A computer controls all the machines, making sure the process does not go over the time limit.

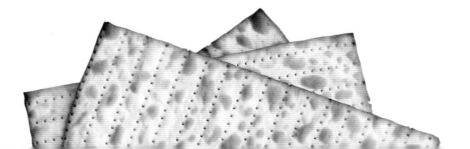

Flour from a kosher-for-Passover mill is delivered into sealed dry storage units . . .

. . . then sent through a tube . . .

. . . directly into the mixer.

Machines roll the dough into a long, flat ribbon . . .

. . . cut it into squares . . .

. . . make holes in it, and separate the pieces so they don't touch each other.

Matzah is baked at

700°F

Conveyer belts take the unbaked matzah into very hot ovens. The matzah bakes for only two minutes.

Tiny elevators take the baked matzah upstairs . . .

35,000 pieces of matzah are made every hour in this factory

. . . where machines seal it in plastic wrap . . .

. . . and pack it into boxes for shipping around the world.

One job can't be done by machine . . . people are needed to check that the matzah is kosher at every step!

Take a closer look

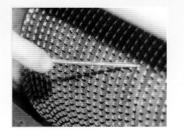

Cleaning the hole-making machine

Factories make other kosher-for-Passover treats, such as cookies and chocolate covered matzah.

Handweaving a matzah cover on a loom.

Matzah covers

During the seder, it is traditional to have three pieces of matzah on the table, under a special cover.

Ethiopian Jews made this beautifully embroidered 3-pocket matzah cover.

Make your own matzah cover

What you need

- 1 piece of fabric, 25 x 25 inches
- Yarn (2 pieces, about 15 inches long)
- Embroidery needle
- Fabric markers and other decorations

Instructions

1. Fold the piece of material in half from bottom to top.
2. Fold it in half again from left to right.
3. Turn the material so the folded edge is at the bottom.
4. Using the needle and yarn, sew along the left side.
5. Then sew along the right side, leaving the top open. This will create 3 pockets for the 3 pieces of matzah.
6. Now decorate it. You can stitch patterns, draw on the material with markers, glue on other pieces of material, or decorate with glitter.

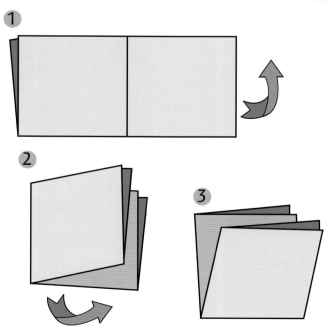

23

Other seder foods

Now we have matzah. Are we ready for Passover? Almost! There are a few other things we need to celebrate the Passover meal.

There are three vegetables on the seder plate. There are different traditions as to which are used. Maror and hazeret are bitter herbs, to remind us of the bitterness of slavery. We use the spicy horseradish root, parsley or other bitter greens for these. Karpas symbolizes the bounty of spring. It can be any leafy green or root vegetable, such as parsley, lettuce or potato.

Charoset is a sweet mixture of fruit, nuts, wine or grape juice and spices. It is made to look like the mortar used by the Israelite slaves.

The Hebrew word seder (סֵדֶר) means "order." Every part of the meal has a special meaning. We eat matzah and other symbolic foods that help us learn about and remember the Exodus from Egypt.

Karpas

Maror

Hazeret

Egg

Charoset

Bone

What do YOU like putting on the seder plate?

As reminders of the offerings brought to the Temple in ancient times, we roast an egg and a bone in the oven. The egg also symbolizes spring.

Traditionally the shank (leg) bone of a sheep is used, but bones from other kosher animals may be used.

Can you match each seder
food with where it comes from?

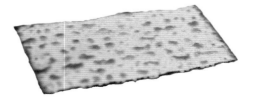

25

Making a seder plate

Artists and crafts people design a wide variety of beautiful and unique seder plates.

Batya Erdstein and her daughter form the seder plate on a pottery wheel.

The finished plate after Batya has glazed, painted and fired it in a kiln.

26

DO IT YOURSELF

Make your own seder plate

What you need

- Paper plate
- 6 cupcake papers
- Crayons
- Stickers

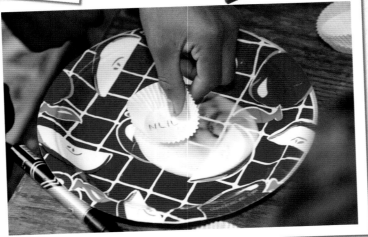

Instructions

1. Glue the cupcake papers onto a paper plate.

2. Label each one.

3. Decorate!

27

The *Seder*: What We Do and Why

Reading the Haggadah

While we eat the seder meal, we read the story of Passover from a book called the Haggadah.

The Hebrew word *Haggadah* means "telling." The Haggadah tells us the order of the Passover seder, with commentaries, stories, pictures and songs.

Dipping twice

We dip the *karpas* in salt water, which reminds us of the tears the Israelites cried as slaves. We also dip the *maror* into the *charoset*, to sweeten the bitterness.

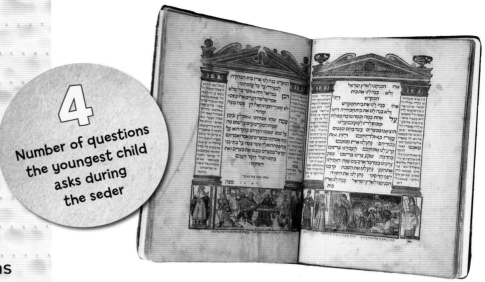

4

Number of questions the youngest child asks during the seder

How do **YOU** think seder night is different from all other nights?

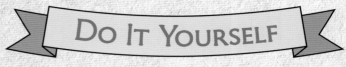

Grow greens to put on the seder plate

1. Fill a planter with potting soil.
2. Sprinkle seeds (such as lettuce, parsley or celery) on the surface of the soil.
3. Cover lightly with more soil.
4. Keep the soil moist.
5. Put the planter where it can get sunlight.

Charoset Recipe

Ingredients

- 3 apples
- 1 cup dried fruit (dates, raisins)
- 1 cup nuts (walnuts, almonds)
- 2 tablespoons sweet red wine or grape juice
- Dash of ground cinnamon, cloves
- 2 tablespoons honey or date syrup

Preparation

1. Peel, core and chop the apples into small pieces.
2. Chop the nuts and dried fruits.
3. Mix the fruit and nuts with wine or grape juice, honey or date syrup, cinnamon and cloves.

The "Hillel sandwich"

At the seder we make a sandwich with matzah, *charoset* and *maror* (lettuce or horseradish). The matzah and *charoset* represent the bricks and mortar used by the Israelites when they had to build for Pharoah. The *maror* reminds us again of the bitterness of slavery.

Four cups of wine

We drink four cups of wine or grape juice during the seder. We fill an extra cup for the Prophet Elijah. During the seder we open the door to symbolically welcome him in.

Grape juice and wine are both made from crushed grapes. If the juice ferments, it becomes wine.

Make a Cup for Elijah

What you need

- Plastic or glass wine cup
- Tissue paper of many colors
- All-purpose glue
- Paintbrush

Instructions

1. Tear the tissue paper into small pieces.
2. Water down the glue in a small dish.
3. Using the paintbrush, put a thin layer of glue on part of the cup.
4. Place a piece of tissue paper over the glue.
5. Cover the paper with more glue.
6. Continue to glue on pieces of tissue paper until the outside of the cup is covered.
7. Allow to dry.

Note: this cup is for decoration only; it cannot be washed in water.

The *Afikomen*

A piece of matzah called the *afikomen* is the last thing we eat at the very end of the meal. There is a tradition that during the seder someone hides the *afikomen*. The children look for it. Whoever finds the *afikomen* gets a treat or prize in exchange for it.

How does eating matzah remind **YOU** of the Passover story?

The seder is not finished until we eat the *afikomen*!

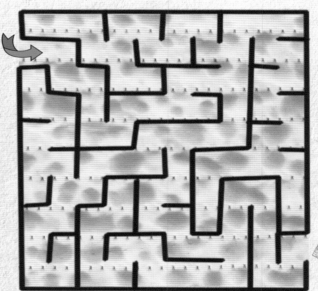

Follow the maze to find the afikomen.

Matzah has few ingredients, but is full of symbolic meaning. We can't celebrate Passover without it.